This book belongs to....

ROARING MAD RILEY

Interior and Cover Designer: Heather Krakora

Art Producer: Hannah Dickerson

Editor: Eun H. Jeong

Illustrations © 2020 Dean Gray

ISBN: Print 978-1-64739-050-1 | eBook 978-1-64739-051-8

R0

Printed in Canada

ROARING MAD RILEY

AN ANGER MANAGEMENT STORY FOR KIDS

WRITTEN BY **Allison Szczecinski, M.Ed.**
ILLUSTRATED BY **Dean Gray**

ROCKRIDGE PRESS

A BRIEF NOTE TO GROWN-UPS

Everyone feels angry at times—it's normal and there is nothing wrong with feeling angry. However, anger can become a challenge when it turns into unsafe and aggressive behavior, and it can be difficult for children to navigate this strong of a feeling.

This book gives you and your child valuable tools and strategies to understand, cope with, and respond to anger. Together, you'll find a story you can relate to, ways to talk about anger that foster open lines of communication, and coping skills for young children to model so they can begin to manage this very big feeling.

After reading the book, we encourage you to keep it close by! Reading it after your child exhibits challenging behavior will help them make connections, and they may find solace in realizing they are not alone.

Riley was happy. She felt like she was floating on clouds.

It was playtime at school,
and she was building a colorful city out of blocks.

It had roads, houses, and trees, just like where Riley lived.
It even had two tall towers that were almost as tall as Riley!

Riley was putting the last block on her bridge
when she heard a *CRASH*!

Oh no! Parker had knocked over her tower!

Riley was mad. Roaring mad!
She could feel her face get very, very hot.
She huffed and puffed. She was breathing so fast!

Her hands curled into fists.
Her shoulders rose up to her ears.
Riley's body felt so tight!

Riley's teacher, Mr. Rex, asked gently,
"Riley, how are you feeling?"

"I am ANGRY!" Riley roared.
She picked up a block and threw it at the other tower.
CRASH! That tower fell down, too.

"It's normal to feel angry sometimes.
Everybody does," said Mr. Rex.
"But even when we feel angry, we need to stay safe."

"When you throw things, you can hurt someone
and you can get hurt, too."

"But Parker knocked down my tower!" Riley shouted.

Parker looked upset. "It was an accident," he said.
"I was moving a tree next to the tower."

But Riley was still roaring mad!

"Sometimes when we feel roaring mad," Mr. Rex said,
"our face gets very, very hot and we breathe very, very fast."

"When we feel this way, we can cool down
by closing our eyes, taking deep breaths from our bellies,
and counting slowly from one to ten."

Riley didn't want to feel hot.
She closed her eyes, took a deep breath from her belly,
and counted slowly to ten.

She felt her face get cooler and her breathing slow down.

"Sometimes when we feel roaring mad,
our body gets very tight," said Mr. Rex.
"When you feel this way, you can shake your hands
and stretch out your arms."

Riley didn't want her body to feel tight.
She shook her hands and stretched her arms.
She could feel her body relax.

"Sometimes when we feel roaring mad,
we want to cry, kick, or shout.
We might even want to throw something."

"When you feel this way, you can think about
something that makes you happy.
I'm thinking of planting roses in my garden."
Mr. Rex closed his eyes and smiled.

Riley didn't want to feel angry. She wanted to smile like Mr. Rex!

She closed her eyes and thought about riding her bike at the playground.

"How are you feeling now, Riley?" asked Mr. Rex.

"I don't feel angry anymore.
But I feel sad that my towers are broken."

"It's okay to feel sad, Riley.
I know you worked hard on those towers," said Mr. Rex.

"But you can build them again,
and you can build them even taller this time."

"I'll help you," Parker said.
"I'm sorry I knocked down your tower."

Riley smiled at Parker. "It's okay," she said.
"I know it was an accident, and I'm not angry anymore.
I'm sorry for throwing the block. I could have hurt you or myself."

"It's okay," said Parker. "Let's build the tower together."

Riley and Parker started building a new tower.
This time, it was even taller than Riley!

Riley was happy again. She felt like she was floating on clouds.

REINFORCEMENTS

Start a Conversation

Discuss the following questions with your child to reinforce the strategies that were introduced in the story. You can also ask these questions as you read the book together, to help your child relate to Riley and make connections to their own experiences with anger.

UNDERSTANDING AND RECOGNIZING ANGER

1. Remember a time you felt angry. Why did you feel angry?

2. How can you tell when someone else feels angry?

3. Why did Riley knock down her block tower?

4. How did Riley's body feel when she was angry? Does your body ever feel that way?

5. What do you do when a toy you like breaks?

MANAGING ANGER

1. Let's take a big, deep breath with our hands on our bellies so that we can feel the air move into our body. How do you feel after taking a big belly breath?

2. Who are some grown-ups you can talk to or ask for help when you are angry?

3. What is your favorite way to calm down when you feel angry?

4. Close your eyes and think of something that makes you feel happy. What did you think about?

5. Why did Riley say, "I'm sorry" to Parker?

Activities for Kids

These extension activities are simple, inviting ways to encourage your child to explore and practice anger management. Engaging in these hands-on activities together after reading the book can help your child make connections to the story in fun and creative ways.

SQUEEZE AND RELEASE

Directions: Ask your child to clasp their hands into two loose fists. Next, direct them to squeeze their fists as tight as they can while counting slowly to three, then release for three counts before tightening again. Have your child try this three times.

Tip: Model the exercise for your child first! Help them by counting to three slowly alongside them as they squeeze their fists. To extend the exercise, you can try Squeeze and Release with different body parts, like your face or your toes.

SMELL THE SOUP, COOL THE SOUP

Directions: Have your child pretend there is a big bowl of soup in front of them. Engage your child's imagination by asking them to pretend to put vegetables and noodles into their soup. Have your child take a big breath in as they smell the noodles and veggies! Once they have taken a deep breath in, tell them the soup is hot and they need to blow on it gently to cool it off. This encourages the child to take a long, slow breath out as they blow.

Tip: To extend the exercise, you can ask your child to think of other hot foods and drinks that can be cooled down, like hot chocolate or macaroni and cheese. They can practice the breathing technique again using different imagery.

COLOR YOUR ANGER

Materials: Paper, crayons, marker

Preparation: Draw with the marker a simple outline of a human body that kids can color in.

Directions: Give the body outline and crayons to the child and ask them to think about a time when they were angry. Then, instruct them to color in the parts of the body that felt "hot" when they felt angry. After they finish coloring, you can ask them what they would do to "cool" down.

Tip: Colors can help make the concept of emotions more concrete for children. Let your child choose whatever color they would like to fill in the "hot" body parts, and use a different color to write down the "cool" down choices they shared.

FEELINGS COLLAGE

Materials: Magazines, scissors, glue, paper

Preparation: Cut out faces of people showing a variety of emotions, including anger, from magazines.

Directions: Have your child sift through and choose pictures to glue on their collage. As they do, have them label the emotions that the pictures are expressing. Ask them, "How can you tell?" Encourage your child to look at the person's eyes, mouth, and other body positions that help show the emotion they're experiencing. When your child glues on a picture of a person feeling angry, ask them to think of ways the person could calm their body.

Tip: Consider relating the pictures with characters from movies, television shows, and other books that your child is familiar with, to help them better connect to the emotion pictures.

RESOURCES FOR GROWN-UPS

Internet Resources

HAND IN HAND
handinhandparenting.org

Hand in Hand supports parents and families by offering skills and tools that help foster healthy relationships.

WE DO LISTEN FOUNDATION
WeDoListen.org

The We Do Listen Foundation seeks to teach emotional regulation in children through print and animated books, lesson plans, videos, and songs.

CONSCIOUS DISCIPLINE
ConsciousDiscipline.com

Conscious Discipline is a social emotional framework that was created by noted childhood education expert Dr. Becky Bailey to help parents and teachers increase their skills for responding to challenging behavior in children.

Books

ANH'S ANGER BY GAIL SILVER

When Anh's grandfather asks him to clean up and come to dinner, Anh becomes angry. His grandfather encourages him to "sit with his anger," and Anh learns how to experience anger in a new way. This book helps reframe the conventional idea of anger into a common emotion that we all experience and can learn from.

VISITING FEELINGS BY LAUREN J. RUBENSTEIN, J.D., Psy.D.

This gorgeously illustrated poetic children's book invites readers to experience emotions with their whole body to better understand how feelings can affect the way their minds think and how their bodies feel.

SODA POP HEAD BY JULIA COOK

Lester is a happy kid, until something seems unfair. Like a shaken-up bottle of soda, when Lester gets angry, he explodes! This book helps children learn new ways to experience anger in a safe way.

EASY TO LOVE, DIFFICULT TO DISCIPLINE BY DR. BECKY BAILEY, Ph.D.

This parenting book, written by a noted childhood education expert, offers specific strategies and tools for parents to be more positive with themselves as they work to support their children's behavior.

ABOUT THE AUTHOR

Allison Szczecinski, M.Ed. is a special education teacher, consultant, mentor, and content creator with over 10 years of field experience. Allison holds her undergraduate and graduate degrees in special education from Illinois State University and the University of Illinois. Currently, Allison lives in Chicago with her family and rescue pets.

ABOUT THE ILLUSTRATOR

Dean Gray is based in South London and completed a B.A. (hons) in graphic design at Leeds Art University before working as a creative designer for Advocate Art Illustration Agency. He now works as a freelancer creating children's book illustration for publishing clients such as Penguin Random House, Scholastic, OUP, Quarto, and Macmillan. He has a character-driven approach to his work, and is passionate about storytelling and creating a character or world that someone can have an emotional connection with. He takes a lot of inspiration from watching films, animation, browsing book shops, and travel.

LetsMakeStuff.co.uk • Instagram: lets_make_stuff